MEDITATE

Happiness Lies Within You

MEDITATE

Happiness Lies Within You

Swami Muktānanda

SIDDHA YOGA®

A SIDDHA YOGA PUBLICATION
PUBLISHED BY SYDA FOUNDATION®
www.siddhayoga.org

Published by SYDA Foundation
PO Box 600, 371 Brickman Road, South Fallsburg, NY 12779-0600, USA

ACKNOWLEDGMENTS

DESIGN: Cheryl Crawford
PRODUCTION EDITOR: Pamela Williams
EDITORIAL CONSULTANTS: Kshama Ferrar and Swami Shāntānanda
COPYEDITOR: Judith Levi
TYPESETTER: Victoria Light
PRINT COORDINATOR: François Simon
TRANSLATION COORDINATOR: Vera Mezina

Original lanaguage: Hindi

Printed in the United States of America

Originally published by State University of New York Press, 1980, 1991
First SYDA Foundation edition 1999

20 19 18 17 3 4 5 6

Library of Congress Cataloging-in-Publication Data.

Muktananda, Swami, 1908-
Meditate : happiness lies within you / Swami Muktananda.—1st SYDA Foundation ed.
p. cm.
Includes bibliographical references and index.
ISBN 0-911307-62-1 (pbk.)
1. Meditation. I. Title.
BL627.M84 1999
294.5'435—dc21 98-32235
CIP

ABOUT THE SYDA FOUNDATION

The SYDA Foundation is a not-for-profit organization that protects, preserves, and facilitates the dissemination of the Siddha Yoga teachings. The SYDA Foundation also guides the philanthropic expressions of the Siddha Yoga path. These include The PRASAD Project, which provides health, education, and sustainable development programs for children, families, and communities in need; and the Muktabodha Indological Research Institute, which contributes to the preservation of the scriptural heritage of India.

NOTE ON THE TEXT

Throughout the text, terms in languages other than English are printed in italics; all proper names are printed in roman type. The standard international transliteration conventions for Sanskrit and modern South Asian languages have been employed. For the reader's convenience a Sanskrit pronunciation guide is included on pages 38–39.

Contents

The Siddha Yoga Lineage ix
Foreword xiv

MEDITATE ON THE SELF 1
ŚAKTIPĀT 10
KNOWLEDGE 12
THE OBJECT OF MEDITATION 16
HOW TO DEAL WITH THE MIND 18
MANTRA 22
ĀSANA 25
PRĀṆĀYĀMA 26
THE PROCESS OF MEDITATION 27
SIDDHA MEDITATION 31
MEDITATION INSTRUCTIONS 35

Guide to Sanskrit Pronunciation 38
Notes 40
Glossary 43
Index 55
Further Study 59

Gurumayi Chidvilāsānanda

The Siddha Yoga Lineage

SIDDHA YOGA is a spiritual path of teachings and practices imparted by the Siddha Yoga Gurus.

GURUMAYI CHIDVILĀSĀNANDA is the Guru of the Siddha Yoga path. Gurumayi is a Siddha Guru, an enlightened meditation Master who has the rare power to awaken within a human being the inner spiritual energy known as Kuṇḍalinī Śakti. Seekers around the world have received this sacred initiation, *śaktipāt dīkṣā,* from Gurumayi and, with her guidance, progress toward the highest spiritual attainment—the unwavering experience of divinity within themselves and all of creation.

Gurumayi received the divine power and authority of the Guru of the Siddha Yoga path from her Guru, Swami Muktānanda, in 1982.

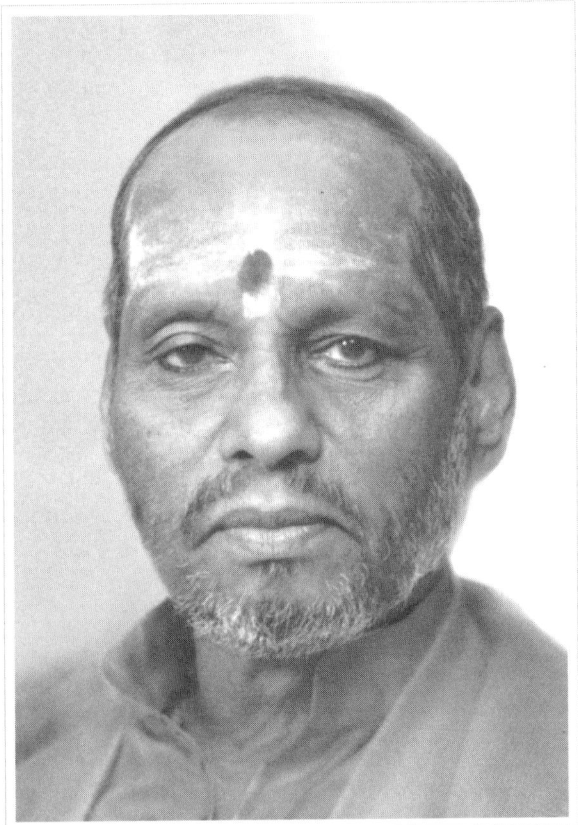

Swami Muktānanda

SWAMI MUKTĀNANDA, affectionately known by his students as Bābā, received *śaktipāt dīkṣā* in 1947 from his Guru, Bhagavān Nityānanda. In 1961, Bhagavān Nityānanda transmitted to Bābā Muktānanda the power and authority to bestow *śaktipāt* initiation.

Bābā gave form and articulation to the Siddha Yoga path, bringing together the teachings that he received from his Guru, the spiritual knowledge and practices from the timeless wisdom of India, and his own direct experience. In the course of three world tours between 1970 and 1982, Bābā imparted the Siddha Yoga teachings and practices to seekers around the globe.

Bhagavān Nityānanda

BHAGAVĀN NITYĀNANDA, also known as Baḍe Bābā, was a *śaktipāt* Guru and a saint widely revered throughout India. He came to settle in the village of Gaṇeśpurī in Mahārāṣṭra state. It was here, in the mid-40s, that Swami Muktānanda became a disciple of Bhagavān Nityānanda. In 1956, Bhagavān Nityānanda asked Swami Muktānanda to establish his own Ashram less than a mile from Gaṇeśpurī. This became the Siddha Yoga Ashram known as Gurudev Siddha Peeṭh.

Foreword

THE TITLE OF THIS BOOK is a powerful spiritual teaching. Swami Muktānanda did not call this book *The Practice of Meditation* nor *How to Meditate*. He titled it *Meditate*, giving us a gentle command, an exhortation to find the happiness that he insists lies in every soul. The book may be small in size, but its message is huge. It offers nothing less than a key to the secret of happiness, and it shows how meditation can lead to the most exalted states of consciousness possible for a human being.

Swami Muktānanda starts from the premise that all human beings want happiness. While we catch glimpses of this happiness when circumstances are favorable, most of us are not able to sustain it during more difficult times. With unimpeachable logic and delightful humor, Swami Muktānanda asks, "When you look at a beautiful picture, where do you feel pleasure, in the picture or in yourself?"[1] He shows us that the source of all good feeling, all happiness, necessarily lies within our own selves. The way to find this joy, he declares, is to meditate, to discover the repository of joy and love that exists in every soul.

Swami Muktānanda was a spiritual teacher of the highest order, one of the rare individuals known in India as a Siddha. Indian scripture describes a Siddha as one who lives in the continuous experience of love. This inner state is the nature of the *ātman*, the Self, so called because it is understood to be the deepest identity, not only of the Siddha, but of every other person as well.

In the eighth-century Vedānta text *Viveka-cūḍāmaṇi* (*The Crest-Jewel of Discrimination*), the sage Saṅkarācārya writes: "Here within the heart, the Self shines in its captivating splendor like a noonday sun."[2] These words are echoed centuries later by the Spanish mystic Teresa of Ávila. Describing the place within where God and the individual soul unite, she writes: "So different from any earthly light is the brightness and light now revealed . . . that, by comparison with it, the brightness of our sun seems quite dim."[3] The congruence of these two writings—and literally hundreds of others—transcends culture, religion, and centuries of time. It points to an ultimate unity at the deepest level of all human consciousness. The inner Self or soul is said to be illuminated with God's light. As Jesus said, "The kingdom of God lies within." And as Swami Muktānanda never tired of repeating: "God dwells within you as you."[4]

Given that we, all of us, have this core of freedom and happiness, within which we can experience the light of God, the question arises, "How do we get there?" Swami Muktānanda gives us a simple answer: "Meditate!" Meditation is the route by which we can access the innermost treasures of our being.

Before I ever heard of Swami Muktānanda, I had learned that meditation provided many practical beneficial effects, and I used it as an adjunct in my psychotherapy practice. People who meditate tend to find more relaxation and peace in their lives. It is also useful for those who want to access more creative or intuitive states of mind. Brain physiologists have noted that the state of meditation—the simple shift of concentration from outer to inner focus—correlates with a slowing down of the brain wave frequency as measured on an electroencephalogram. The same kind of slowing of brain waves occurs as we fall asleep or as we day-dream and can be associated with heightened intuition and creativity. For example, Francis Crick found the answer to the structure of DNA in a dream; Anton Bruckner woke up with the scherzo of his seventh symphony resounding in his mind; and Albert Einstein derived one of his concepts of relativity from a day-dream in which he imagined angels traveling down a light beam. Peacefulness, creativity, good feeling, intuition, an increased ability to focus—these all correlate with a slower brain rhythm that can be fostered and developed in meditation.

As a psychiatrist, I had long been familiar with such effects of meditation, as well as with different theories of the nature of the self. The notion of full Self-realization seemed like a worthy goal, and yet I assumed, like many of my colleagues, that it was not finally achievable, that it was an ideal state beyond the horizon of human capacity. Though I recognized the value of meditation, I did not believe that it was possible to experience the highest Self, the divine essence of the soul that is described by the mystical traditions of both the East and West.

Though I recognized the wisdom of striving to be happy independent of one's circumstances, I had certainly never met anyone who had fully achieved this state of mind. Enlightened Masters appeared to be mythical beings from the past, and I thought that if they ever existed, they were certainly now extinct. Then, in 1988, someone told me that there were indeed living Masters and that he had in fact met one—the heir to Swami Muktānanda's spiritual lineage, Gurumayi Chidvilāsānanda. Interested and skeptical, I decided to visit the Siddha Yoga Ashram in the Catskill Mountains of upstate New York.

Two months later, I was sitting in a large hall of Shree Muktānanda Ashram, knowing that Gurumayi would enter at some unspecified time. The room was filled with people, and various speakers explained different aspects of yoga, their images projected from a podium at the front of the room onto two huge video screens. I closed my eyes for a while, during which time I suddenly felt a palpable surge of energy move through my body, starting in my head and moving down through the soles of my feet. Looking up, I saw a woman dressed in orange robes walking down a center aisle. I surmised that this was Gurumayi. Later that day, I noted that she seemed to be surrounded by an invisible energy field. Within that field, I experienced heightened awareness and a sense of joyful well-being and love, as if they radiated from her presence. In fact, I had never felt so happy in all my life. I was quite surprised. There was something going on here that did not fit the parameters of my experience of people nor my medical and psychological training. I began to wonder if my assumptions about the limits of what is possible in life were completely accurate.

I read this book two days later, and the day following, I had an experience of the magic that Swami Muktānanda describes in these pages. Sitting in meditation, my posture and breath steady, I became aware that I could see on an inner mental screen an image of Swami Muktānanda himself, looking serene and kind. This image was nothing like a photograph; Swami Muktānanda appeared to be fully alive and present. To my surprise, I saw him lean forward. With his face only a few inches from mine, he gently blew into my mouth. Before I had a chance to react, the vision of Swami Muktānanda's form had assumed such gigantic proportions that, by comparison, my body was half the size of his thumb. As he continued to blow gently, I floated right through his mouth—and found myself in the vast starry expanse of the cosmos. It seemed I was enveloped in an infinite universe of love, all appearing to be within Swami Muktānanda's own form. I had never felt such love before, nor did I know it existed. Later, as I thought about the experience, I saw that this vast inner universe of love, while appearing to be within his form, was of course all within my own consciousness, just as he had said.

After this experience, my life changed in ways it is difficult to fathom. I wept tears of joy that day, and in the weeks and years that followed, I have found myself more loving with my wife and sons, with my friends and clients, and also with people I have never seen before, people I might encounter while shopping or walking down the street. I began to realize that the source of love is not in the circumstances or the people around me, but within my own inner being. A year after that meditation experience, I learned that Swami Muktānanda, during his lifetime, had sometimes initiated seekers into the experience of the Self by gently blowing breath into the mouth or nose.

As I studied and practiced the meditation prescribed by Swami Muktānanda, the benefits I had previously ascribed to it—enhanced relaxation, focus, creativity—seemed tame compared to what I now knew was possible. "We do not meditate only to relax a little and experience some peace," says Swami Muktānanda. "We meditate to unfold our inner being."[5] Meditation, he says, can take us to the very core of our own divine nature, to the recognition that "God dwells within you as you." It is in the inner heart that true happiness, independent of the circumstances of our lives, is found. This is the state of transcendence.

The highest goal in meditation, Swami Muktānanda says, is to reach this transcendent state, known in the Indian scriptures as *turīya,* or the fourth and highest state of Consciousness. Swami Muktānanda explains the Vedantic categorization of four different planes of awareness: the waking state, the dream state, the deep sleep state, and the transcendent state. The first three of these states correspond with what has been described recently by scientific specialists in sleep and dreaming. The brain wave patterns of these three states, as measured on an electroencephalogram, are remarkably distinct. While the distinction between dreaming and deep sleep has been recognized in the West only for a relatively brief period, the difference between the two states has been established in Indian psychology for millennia.

The ancient Indian seers had the advantage of being in touch with a highly tuned and very subtle inner awareness that allowed them to thoroughly understand the phases and gradations of Consciousness itself. This refined discernment, an aspect of the fourth transcendental state of Consciousness, is also known as the Self.

Swami Muktānanda explains that the Self is the eternal witness of all things. When we are fully attuned to the Self as this witnessing consciousness, we are in the fourth great plane of awareness. This is a subtle state, not as yet measurable by scientific instruments. During Swami Muktānanda's second world tour in 1974, a brain wave researcher once asked him to come to his laboratory; he wanted to know what the brain waves of a Self-realized being looked like. Swami Muktānanda laughed and told him that Consciousness is too subtle to be captured by a machine. He added that if the researcher wanted to know what a meditator's experience is like, he could come to *his* laboratory and experience meditation for himself. In the subtle spiritual plane, in this fourth dimension of awareness, we move beyond what can be verified by the five senses or any form of instrumentation. But if we are willing to experiment on ourselves, says Swami Muktānanda, we can begin to experience the delight of the ineffable.

Swami Muktānanda invites us to undertake such an experiment in this book. He does not offer a set of fixed rules on how to meditate. Instead he shows us how to create the right atmosphere so that meditation, which always transcends the human will, can occur naturally. This atmosphere is brought into being, he explains, by four primary practices.

The first practice is to focus the mind on an inner object. Swami Muktānanda explains that we all have the capacity to concentrate on an object or a task. The only difference in meditation is that the focus is shifted within. It is this quietened state of mind that is conducive to meditation. We can focus on the space between the eyebrows, or on the heart center, or on an image of beauty or sanctity. Once again, however, Swami Muktānanda invites us to take a huge leap further. While it is true that focusing within quietens and readies the mind for meditation, we can go much deeper when we realize that "the mind becomes like that on which it meditates."[6] In other words, our minds, and ultimately our lives, are governed by what we choose to focus on. This fact has been noted by the scriptures of many religions. The Bible says: "As a man thinketh in his heart, so he is," while the *Maitrī Upaniṣad* puts it this way: "What a person thinks is what he becomes."[7] In the early 1900s, the psychologist Émile Coué affirmed that whenever attention is concentrated on an idea over and over again, that idea spontaneously tends to realize itself. From this statement followed the Western psychological method of using affirmations to condition the mind positively.

Since we become what we meditate on, we might as well, says Swami Muktānanda, meditate on the very highest, which is the divine essence that lies within. But how can we focus on that which by its very nature is beyond rational conception or mental representation? The answer, Swami Muktānanda explains, is to understand the Self as the witness of the mind. It is the Self that knows that we have dreamed a dream, and it is the Self that says *my* mind. In other words, the Self is the *I* that is beyond the mind, and from this vantage point we do not have to battle the mind—a problem that many meditators complain of. We can simply watch our thoughts with compassion.

The second practice is repetition of a sacred formula of words known as a mantra. While I was aware of the power of ordinary words to affect someone's state (for instance, how easy it is for us to hurt or uplift others through the words we choose), it was only after I received the Siddha Yoga mantra that I became aware of the even more subtle and powerful effects that words can have. A mantra affects us on many levels. It increases our focus on the highest aspect of ourselves, the Self, and gives us a simple means to do so. More importantly, the sacred sounds and syllables employed in mantras are the subtle vibration of the Self in the form of sound, and are empowered to directly grant us the experience of the Self. The mantra that Swami Muktānanda offers us here is *Oṁ Namaḥ Śivāya,* which means—freely translated—"I honor the divinity within." The successful practice of mantra repetition requires the knowledge that the "I" who honors, and the divinity that is honored—Śiva, or supreme Consciousness—are one and the same.

The third practice Swami Muktānanda describes here is *āsana,* or posture. The correlation between body posture and state of mind is well known in many fields of medicine and psychotherapy. A slumped posture not only denotes a depressed state, but can actually cause a depressed state. Conversely, an erect, though not rigid, body posture both denotes and causes a state of peaceful exhilaration. The ancient practitioners of meditation knew this correlation and advised a steady erect posture for meditation. They also knew that when the body is maintained in this steady position, it gives the best alignment of the energy system, of the subtle juncture points and channels known as *cakras* and *nāḍīs,* and hence the best possible flow of spiritual energy. In addition, the repeated practice of a meditation position sets up a useful habitual response—meditation begins to occur naturally just from its association with a particular posture. *Āsana* is another way of setting the ambience, the right conditions, so that the magic of meditation can occur of its own accord.

The fourth practice is to maintain a steady natural breath. The steady breath is associated both with greater feeling and with an enhanced connection to our own subtler energy systems. The mind and the breath are also deeply connected. Fast, shallow breathing, for example, tends to accentuate anxiety and restlessness. As the breath becomes natural and quiet, so the mind quietens in harmony.

All of these four practices presented by Swami Muktānanda help still the body and the mind. It is when the outer realms of thought and bodily activity are quiet that the subtler realms—the inner universe—can be discovered. This "inner universe," Swami Muktānanda tells us, "is much greater than the outer universe; it is so vast that the entire outer cosmos can be kept in just one corner of it."[8] When you consider the known size of the visible universe, this is quite a statement! If I hadn't caught a glimpse of this in my own experience, I might well not have believed it.

Meditate is Swami Muktānanda's encouragement to us to go so much further than we ever knew we could. It was his explicit wish for all of us that we turn within to the Self of infinite love, so that we can experience this for ourselves and so that we can relate to others from that inner place of love and respect. As Swami Muktānanda's own teacher, Bhagavān Nityānanda, said: "The Heart is the hub of all sacred places. Go there and roam."

Dr. Richard Gillett
South Fallsburg, New York
September 1998
Revised July 2014

Dr. Gillett studied medicine at Cambridge University in England, specializing in psychiatry and becoming a member of the Royal College of Psychiatrists. He is the author of a number of professional articles and of two books: *Overcoming Depression,* which was published by Dorling and Kindersley, and *Change Your Mind, Change Your World,* published by Simon and Schuster.

MEDITATE

Happiness Lies Within You

MEDITATE ON THE SELF

IN THE UPANIṢADS there is a question: What do human beings want? The answer is that we want happiness. Everything we do, we do for the sake of happiness. We seek that happiness through our work, through our friends and family, through art and science, through food, drink, and entertainment. For happiness, we perform all the activities of daily life, and this is why we keep expanding our material world.

Inside us lies divine happiness, the same happiness we are looking for in the world. If we think about the joy we derive from different activities, we will realize that we experience happiness not in the activities, but within ourselves. For example, when you look at a beautiful picture, where do you feel pleasure, in the picture or in yourself? When you eat a delicious meal, do you experience satisfaction in the food or in yourself? When you meet a friend and feel joy, is that joy in your friend or in yourself? The truth is that the joy you find in all these things is simply a reflection of the joy of your own inner Self.

The testimony for this is our sleep. At the end of every day, no matter how much we have eaten or drunk or earned or enjoyed, we are exhausted. All we want to do is to go into our bedroom, turn off the light, and take refuge in a blanket. During sleep, we are completely alone. We do not want our wife, our husband, our friends, our possessions. We do not eat anything, we do not earn anything, we do not enjoy anything. Yet while we are sleeping, the weariness of our waking hours is removed independently, by the strength of our own spirit. In the morning when we wake up, we feel completely rested.

This is an experience that we have every day. If we think carefully about why we become exhausted from everything we do during the day and why we get so much peace from sleep, we will understand that the real source of our contentment is not eating or drinking or anything outside ourselves, but is within. During the day, the mind turns outward. However, in the sleep state the mind takes some rest in the Self, and it is this which removes our fatigue. Absorbed in the little bliss of sleep, we forget the pains of the waking state. If we were to go just beyond sleep and enter into the state of meditation, we would be able to drink the nectar of love and happiness that lies in the heart.

That nectar is what we are looking for in all the activities of the outer world. What we are really seeking is the supreme Truth, and through meditation we can experience that Truth vibrating in the form of sublime happiness in the heart.

Truly speaking, a human being is divine. It is only our wrong understanding that keeps us small. We think of ourselves as the body. We think that we are a certain physical structure, with hands, feet, legs, and eyes. We think of ourselves as a man or a woman, as belonging to a particular class or country. We identify ourselves with our thoughts, our talents, our good or bad actions. But none of these things is what we are.

Within us is a being who knows all the actions of the body and the mind and remains untouched by all of them. In the *Bhagavad-gītā*, Lord Kṛṣṇa says: "Arjuna, this body is called a field, and the one who knows it is called the knower of the field."[1]

The one who knows the field must be different from the field. For example, one who says "my book" must be different from the book; one who says "my table" must be different from the table. In the same way, one who says "my body" must be different from the body; one who says "my mind" must be different from the mind. Who is that being who observes the activities of our waking hours? At night when we go to sleep, that being does not sleep, but stays awake and in the morning reports to us on our dreams. Who is that knower? In the *Gītā*, Kṛṣṇa answers this question: "O Arjuna, I am the knower of all these fields."[2]

The one who lives in the body, but who is apart from the body as the knower of it, is our real Self. That Self is beyond the body, beyond the mind, beyond distinctions of name, color, and sex. It is the pure "I," the original I-consciousness that has been with us since we came into the world. We have superimposed different notions onto that I-awareness, notions like "I am black," "I am white," "I am a man," "I am a woman," "I am American," "I am Indian." Yet when we wipe away those superimpositions, that "I" is nothing but pure Consciousness, and it is of the form of bliss. It was with the awareness of that "I" that the great Śaṅkarācārya proclaimed, *ahaṁ brahmāsmi,* "I am the Absolute."[3] That "I" is God, and we meditate to know That directly. As we see it more and more, we become transformed.

There are many techniques that are supposed to lead us to God, but of all these, meditation is the one recognized by all the saints and sages, because only in meditation can we see the inner Self directly. That which lives in the heart cannot be found in books. If we look for it in churches and temples, we cannot find it. Logical reasoning and the ability to give great lectures are of no use either. Since that being is our innermost Consciousness, it is necessary for us to turn within to have a direct experience of it.

There was a time when I was addicted to reading the scriptures. One day I went to see my Guru with a book under my arm. He said, "Muktānanda, come here. What is that?"

"It's an Upaniṣad," I replied.

"Do you know how this book was made?" he asked me. "It was made by a brain. The brain may make any number of books, but a book cannot make a brain. You had better throw it away and meditate."

So I threw the book away and began to meditate. This makes perfect sense. When the Self is within, why should we look for knowledge of it somewhere else? As long as we do not realize the Self within, we cannot find true peace. We can never be happy, no matter how much we have in the outside world. So meditation has the highest importance; it is necessary for everyone.

The Upaniṣads say that everything in the universe is in meditation. The earth is held in position by meditation, fire burns through the power of meditation, water flows through the power of meditation, and the wind blows through the power of meditation. Through meditation, the ancient sages discovered the various laws of society and how to govern so that everything functioned smoothly. In the same way, the secrets of the ancient sciences were revealed to these sages. Through meditation, they accomplished great tasks.

Meditation is universal. It is not the property of any particular sect or cult. It does not belong to the East or to the West, nor does it belong to Hinduism, Buddhism, or Sufism. Meditation is everyone's property, just as sleep is everyone's property: it belongs to humanity. Meditation is not something difficult or strange. All of us, in our daily lives, are already familiar with it. Without meditation, a doctor could not diagnose a disease, nor could a lawyer prepare a brief, nor a student pass an examination. All our arts and skills, from driving a car to cooking a meal to painting a picture to solving a mathematical problem, are perfected through the power of concentration, which is nothing but meditation. However, these are external forms of meditation. When we turn our attention within and focus on our inner being just as we focus on external objects, we are meditating on the Self.

Meditation is such a great purifier that it washes away the sins of countless lifetimes and removes all the impurities and tensions that beset the mind. Meditation rids us of disease and makes us more skillful at everything we do. Through meditation, our inner awareness expands, and our understanding of inner and outer things becomes steadily deeper. Through meditation, we travel to different inner worlds and have innumerable inner experiences. Above all, meditation stills the mind—which constantly wanders, which constantly causes suffering—and establishes us forever in the state of supreme peace, which is independent of any external factors. Ultimately, meditation makes us aware of our own true nature. It is this awareness that removes all suffering and delusion, and this awareness comes only when we see, face-to-face, our own inner Self.

If even once we could see the Self as separate from the body, we would understand that the body does not bind us, that the pains and pleasures of the body do not affect us. According to the seers of Vedānta, pain and pleasure affect only a person who does not know the inner Self. Even in daily life, we know that we experience physical pain and pleasure only for a certain length of time and only in a certain state of consciousness; we do not experience them at all times or in all states. For example, if a person has a boil on his hand, it hurts during the day, but as soon as he goes to sleep, he stops feeling the pain. A person may have a nightmare in which he sees a tiger rushing at him, and he may become frightened and scream, "Save me, save me!" But when he awakens, the tiger is nowhere around, and he realizes that he has only been dreaming.

So the pleasures and pains of the dream state do not reach the waking state. In the same way, the state of meditation is beyond the pleasures and pains of the waking, dream, and deep-sleep states. In meditation, we become the witness of all our states. This is the state of God, of the inner Self, and through meditation we can attain that state because it is within us. When we pass from dream to waking consciousness, our understanding of ourselves changes. In the same way, when we reach the state of the Self, we understand ourselves differently: we understand that we are divine.

There was a great being named Hazrat Bāyazīd Bistāmī. He was a Sūfī who used to pray and meditate continually. As his meditation became deeper, he reached a state in which he began to proclaim, "I am God, I am God." One who has not experienced that state may find it hard to understand, so I will explain with a simple analogy. You know from your own experience that your idea of yourself keeps changing as your consciousness changes. A policeman, as long as he is an ordinary policeman, will keep saying, "I am a policeman." When he becomes a captain, he will stop saying, "I am a policeman," and say, "I am a captain." And when he becomes a commissioner, he will say, "I am a commissioner." As long as a person is studying, he says, "I am a student," but when he finishes his studies and begins to teach, he says, "I am a teacher." The same "I" is experiencing all these states. When that "I" which identifies itself with the body in the waking state, saying, "This body is mine" or "I am a policeman" or "I am an American," passes from the level of waking consciousness to the highest, subtlest level of consciousness, it attains this awareness: "I am God." That understanding emanates from the deepest place inside us.

When a river flows into the ocean and becomes one with the ocean, it is no longer a river; it is the ocean. In the same way, Hazrat Bistāmī would reach a state in which he would experience himself as all-pervasive Consciousness, the highest Truth, and he would shout, "I am God." He did not know what was happening to him, and he could not pass into this state at will.

Although he was a great being, Bistāmī's teachings had always been the orthodox teachings of Muslim priests. He would tell his students, "Pray to God; be forgiven for your sins. God is somewhere up above." So when Bistāmī began to shout during meditation, "I am God, I am God," his students were shocked. When he came out of his room, they surrounded him and cried, " Bistāmī, you are guilty of a terrible heresy! We cannot understand what is happening."

Bistāmī said, "Please tell me, what sin have I committed?"

The students explained, "We could hear you exclaiming from inside your room, 'I am God, I am God.' How can a human being, who is corrupt and sinful, be God? That goes against the holy law of Islam."

"I am not really to blame for this," Bistāmī told them. "When I am in meditation, I am not in control of what I say. If you hear me say these things again, you can punish me in any way you like."

The students agreed. After about a week's time, Bistāmī again sat in meditation. This time he began to shout louder than ever, "I am God, I am God, I am God! This earth has come from me. I am the mountains and all the oceans. I flow as water in the rivers. I am everywhere. I am in the West and the East; I am in the North and the South; I am above and below."

When the students heard Bistāmī shouting in this way, they thought he had become completely insane and rushed to get weapons in order to silence him. As soon as Bistāmī came out of his room after meditation, the students grabbed him and began to beat him.

There was only one of him, and there were so many students. What could he do? So once again, he sat down. The moment he touched the ground, he glided into meditation and began to proclaim, "I am God, I am God. Whatever there is has emanated from me. Fire cannot burn me, water cannot wet me, and bullets cannot kill me. I am in that state which is beyond everything. I am the highest of the high. Death cannot come anywhere near me. I am That which is the supreme Lord."

As the students were stoning and beating Bistāmī, an amazing thing happened. The punishment they were inflicting began to rebound onto themselves. The student who had been hitting Bistāmī's head found his own head being hit. The one who had struck his arms found his own arms hurt. Another who had been beating his legs found his own legs broken. Finally, for their own sake, the students stopped beating Bistāmī and sat down.

Bistāmī was still shouting, "I am God, I am God," but the students did not want to take another chance. They sat at a respectful distance, not daring to go anywhere near him. After a while, Bistāmī came out of meditation, and the students said to him, "Sir, we don't understand what has happened. Our legs and arms are bleeding. Our heads are broken. We thought we were hitting you, but we ended up hitting ourselves."

Bistāmī said, "When I was in meditation, when I was in that state, I was no longer Bistāmī. I was the highest goal of your religion. I was all-pervasive, and if anyone hits a being in such a state, it is like hitting one's own Self. That is why the blows bounced back onto you."

This is the state that we are supposed to attain in meditation. We do not meditate only to relax a little and experience some peace. We meditate to unfold our inner being. The *Bṛhaj-jābāla Upaniṣad* says: Through meditation, we reach a place where the wind does not blow, where the heat of the sun does not reach, where death cannot penetrate.[4] This is the country of eternal bliss. If a yogi becomes established there, he becomes liberated. Death cannot touch him.

ŚAKTIPĀT

MEDITATION ON THE SELF is not difficult. The real secret of meditation is *śaktipāt,* the inner awakening that takes place through contact with a Siddha Guru. Within every human being lies a great and divine energy. The Indian scriptures refer to it by different names, such as *śakti* (supreme energy) or *citi* (universal Consciousness), and when it resides within a human body, this conscious energy is known as *kuṇḍalinī.* This inner power is the same creative force that is responsible for the creation, sustenance, and withdrawal of the world.

The *Pratyabhijñā-hṛdayam,* one of the essential texts of the great spiritual philosophy Kashmir Shaivism, describes this energy in an aphorism: "Universal Consciousness creates this universe in total freedom."[5]

Contemporary scientists are becoming aware that the basis of the universe is energy. They are discovering what the sages of India have known for millennia: that it is Consciousness which forms the ground, or canvas, on which the material universe is drawn. In fact, the entire world is the play of this energy. Within its own being, by its own free will, it manifests this universe of diversities and becomes all the forms and shapes we see around us. This energy pervades every particle of the universe, from the supreme Principle to the tiniest insect, and performs infinite functions. Yet even though it becomes the world, this Consciousness remains untouched and free of stain.

Just as this energy pervades the universe, it permeates the human body, filling it from head to toe. It is this *śakti* that carries on all our life functions. It becomes the *prāṇa* and *apāna,* the incoming and outgoing breaths. It is the power that makes our heart beat and causes the blood to flow in our veins. In this way, this conscious energy powers our bodies.

However, in its inner spiritual aspect, the energy ordinarily lies dormant. The awakening of this latent inner energy is essential for all of us, because only when it is activated and unfolds within us are we truly able to experience the Self. This inner Kuṇḍalinī Śakti resides at a subtle energy center known as the *mūlādhāra-cakra,* located at the base of the spine. The awakening of this energy is the beginning of a subtle inner process, leading ultimately to the state of union with the Self.

There are several ways this awakening can take place. However, the easiest is through *śaktipāt,* the transmission of energy from a fully Self-realized spiritual Master. In *śaktipāt,* just as a lit candle lights an unlit one, one's inner energy is kindled by the fully unfolded energy of the Guru. Then one no longer has to make an effort to meditate. Meditation comes spontaneously on its own.

KNOWLEDGE

THE UPANIṢADS TEACH that we cannot attain the Self simply by doing good actions or by performing rituals. We can attain the Self only through direct knowledge; it is that knowledge which makes us one with God.[6] When our dormant *śakti* is awakened, this knowledge arises very naturally, and we are able to see the Self.

If we had the right understanding, we could experience God right away. If the sun is out and we go outside, we see it immediately. How much time does it take to see the sun when it is shining in the sky? In the same way, the light of God is shining within us all the time. How long should it take us to perceive that light which shines at every moment in our hearts? This is why the scriptures say that we meditate not to attain God but to perceive the God who is already within us. Kashmir Shaivism says that if one does not already have something, trying to attain it is of no use, since one can lose it in the future. The *Vijñāna Bhairava,* one of the revealed texts of Kashmir Shaivism, teaches that God, the Self, is present in all one's inner feelings, one's inner understanding, and one's inner knowledge. He is closer than anyone or anything; it is only because of our weak understanding that we are not able to know him.

The sage Vasiṣṭha told Lord Rāma, "It is very easy to see God. You can see him in the time it takes to blink your eyes. Yet many lifetimes have gone by, and you still haven't seen him."[7]

The Upaniṣads teach that God is of the form of *sat, cit,* and *ānanda*: absolute existence, Consciousness, and bliss. *Sat* means "Truth," that which exists in all places, in all things, and at all times. If Truth were not omnipresent, it would not be the Truth; it would not have absolute existence. For example, if you are in New York, you are real in New York, but since you are not in Los Angeles, you are not real there. But God, being *sat,* is not bound by place or time, nor is he restricted to one particular object. What object is there that is not Śiva?[8] What country is there where Śiva is not? That Consciousness, that God, exists in his fullness in everything. Being present in everything, he is present in our hearts, and we can find him there.

The next element is *cit. Cit* means "Consciousness" or "that which illuminates everything." *Cit* is the light of the Self, which destroys ignorance. *Cit* makes us aware of all outer objects, and it also makes us aware that God exists inside. Moreover, if we think that God does not exist because we have not seen him, it is *cit* that illuminates that understanding. *Cit* is the discloser of the knowledge that something exists or does not exist. *Cit* is that which illuminates all places and all things at all times; therefore, *cit* also illuminates our inner being.

The final element is *ānanda. Ānanda* is absolute bliss, the bliss of Consciousness. This bliss is far superior to the pleasure that arises from seeing a beautiful form, hearing a melodious sound, tasting delicious food, or experiencing the softness of a touch. The pleasure born of looking at a beautiful form depends on that form, and if the form disappears, the bliss also disappears. The pleasure that comes from listening to a melodious sound depends on that sound, and if the sound disappears, the pleasure also disappears. In the same way, the pleasure born of a soft touch depends on that touch, and when the touch is no more, the pleasure also dies. But *ānanda* does not depend on any external factor. It arises, unconditioned, from within. When the mind and intellect come close to the Self, they are able to experience bliss. It is to attain that bliss, to establish ourselves in that bliss, that we meditate. When we attain the light of the Self within ourselves, that light emerges as supreme Love.

So God, the Self, is of the form of *sat, cit,* and *ānanda.* Being *sat, cit,* and *ānanda,* he pervades everywhere, and therefore we can see him anywhere. The real question is: do we want to see God as he is or as we want him to be? If we want to see him as he is, he is manifest; he is not concealed. If the intellect is sufficiently subtle and refined, we can experience him instantly. This is why the sages agree that in the attainment of the Self, understanding and knowledge are more important than techniques of meditation. Mere spiritual practice will not help us to know God. People think that, by pursuing different practices, they can attain him. They take a course here and do not attain anything; they take a course there and do not attain anything. They take course after course, and the more expensive the course, the more they rush to enroll in it. However, the object of spiritual practice, or *sādhanā*, is not attained by these practices. Kashmir Shaivism speaks of the net of *sādhanā* and says that spiritual practices cannot illuminate the Self any more than a pot can illuminate the sun.[9]

Once Sheikh Nasruddīn woke up early in the morning. There was no moon; it was pitch black. He called his disciple Mahmūd and asked him to go outside and see if the sun had risen.

Mahmūd went out and came back a moment later. "O Nasruddīn Sāhib, it is very dark outside. I cannot see the sun at all."

"You idiot!" shouted Nasruddīn. "Haven't you got the sense to use a flashlight?"

To expect a mere spiritual discipline to illuminate the indwelling God is like trying to see the sun with a flashlight. If the sun has really risen, one does not have to use a flashlight to see it. The flashlight cannot shine beside the sun, nor can darkness bear to remain after the sun has come up. In the same way, no technique can reveal the Self. Nothing can illuminate the Self, because it is the Self that illuminates everything.

It is only because our inner instruments are not refined

enough to approach the Self that we have to meditate. The *Yoga-sūtra* of Patañjali, an authoritative scripture on meditation, explains that although the Self is always blazing within us, the restlessness of the mind acts as a barrier. According to Patañjali, when the mind becomes still and turns inward, we immediately perceive the Self.[10]

THE OBJECT OF MEDITATION

THE FIRST QUESTION THAT ARISES when we sit for meditation is: what should we meditate on? People meditate on all kinds of objects and recommend many different techniques. Maharṣi Patañjali speaks of concentration, or *dhāraṇā,* in which one focuses one's attention on a particular object in order to still and focus the mind.[11] One can concentrate on the heart, on the space between the eyebrows, or on other centers of the body. One can also focus on a being who has risen above passion and attachment; as the mind clings to such a being, it will take on his qualities. In fact, Patañjali says that one may concentrate wherever the mind finds satisfaction.

However, the best object of meditation is the inner Self. When the Self is the goal of meditation, why should we choose another object? If we want to experience the Self, we should meditate on the Self. If we want to know God, we should meditate on God. The mind becomes like that on which it meditates. The poet-saint Sundardās sang:

The mind that always thinks of a woman
  takes on a woman's form.
The mind that is always angry
  burns in the fire of anger.
The mind that contemplates illusion
  falls into the well of illusion.
The mind that continually takes refuge in the Supreme
  eventually becomes That.[12]

For this reason, we should choose for the object of meditation that which is our true nature. When we meditate on the Self, not only do we experience the Self, we become the very form of the Self.

Once a seeker asked a sage, "Who is that God on whom I can meditate?" The sage replied, "God is the witness of your mind." That witness is the goal of meditation. The Upaniṣads say, "It lives in the mind, but the mind cannot know it, because the mind is its body."[13] The Self is the witness of the mind, and it is also the source of the mind. In the *Kena Upaniṣad*, there is a statement: "That is God who makes the mind think, but who can never be apprehended by the mind."[14] One whom the mind can think about cannot be the supreme Truth, because that Self is the motive power behind all the movements of the mind. The Self makes the mind think, the imagination fantasize, and the ego constantly prattle, "I, I, I." In the same way, God is the one through whose inspiration we meditate.

In the *Gītā*, Lord Kṛṣṇa says: "O Arjuna, That shines through all our senses yet is without the senses. It supports all the senses yet remains apart from them. It experiences the different qualities of nature yet remains detached from them."[15]

Who is that being who knows all the positive and negative thoughts that come and go in the mind? During meditation, when we have inner problems, that being perceives all of them. That being is of the form of knowledge. It is that which makes us know everything. For example, in meditation, something comes up inside. First we become aware of it; we have the knowledge that it is arising. Then we know exactly what it is. We identify it as a good or bad thought. That which makes us aware of the existence of something and of exactly what it is, is nothing but the Self. It is that pure awareness that is the Self, not our good or bad thoughts. Within and without, whatever action takes place, whatever we do, it is the Self that makes us aware that it is happening. This awareness is constantly there, inside us. It is the pure I-consciousness, without form or attribute. Just as it knows everything inside and outside, it knows itself. To know this knower is true meditation.

HOW TO DEAL WITH THE MIND

THE HIGHEST MEDITATION is the state of complete inner stillness. In that state, not a single thought arises in the mind. However, most people cannot attain this state of stillness right away. For that reason, it is of the greatest importance for a meditator to understand how to deal with the mind.

Most people who meditate make the same mistake. When they sit for meditation, they do not focus on the Self. Instead, they run after the mind, trying to find out what it is doing. People always complain to me, "When I try to meditate, different thoughts keep rushing into my mind." Sometimes their minds are filled with anger, sometimes with hatred, sometimes with lust. At one moment, they are thinking of someone they love; at another moment, they are remembering their past bad actions and are filled with remorse. The more they try to obliterate thoughts from the mind, the more thoughts rush in. Instead of meditating on the Self, they find themselves like the seeker who found himself meditating on a monkey.

Once there was a seeker who went to a Guru to learn meditation. The Guru said, "I will choose an auspicious time for your initiation, and then I will call you." When the auspicious hour came, the Guru called the seeker and made all the proper arrangements for the initiation. After he had completed all the parts of the ritual, he said, "I am going to give you an important instruction. When you sit for meditation, first bow in all four directions and begin to repeat your mantra. But remember one thing. Whatever you do, don't think of a monkey."

"Why on earth would I think of a monkey?" asked the disciple. "I never thought of a monkey in my life. I don't care about monkeys; I care only about God."

When the initiation was over, the young man returned home, spread out a mat, and sat on it, facing east. He took a sip of holy water and bowed in all four directions, and then he began to think about his Guru's last instruction. "What was it my Guru said? Oh yes, 'Don't think of a monkey.' " Immediately a monkey appeared in his mind.

The seeker was upset. "Where did that monkey come from?" he wondered. He opened his eyes and took another sip of holy water. Again he recalled what his Guru had said: "Don't think of a monkey." Once again, a monkey stood before him.

The seeker made three, four, five more attempts to meditate and each time was confronted with the monkey. Finally he rushed back to his Guru. "O Guru, O holy seer, what shall I do? Until I came to you, I didn't know what a monkey looked like, and now, when I sit for meditation, a monkey is all I can see."

This is what happens when we try to subdue the mind forcibly in meditation. Instead of worrying about the thoughts in the mind, instead of trying to erase the thoughts from the mind, it would be much better if we tried to understand the nature of the mind. What is the mind? The mind has no independent existence. The Upaniṣads say that the Self has itself become the mind. The mind is nothing but a contracted form of the supreme Consciousness that has created the universe. The *Pratyabhijñā-hṛdayam* explains this in an aphorism: "Citi herself, descending from the plane of pure consciousness, becomes the mind by contracting in accordance with the object perceived."[16] This means that when Consciousness descends from its status as pure Consciousness and assumes limitations, it becomes the stuff of the mind.

This is easy to understand if we think about what actually constitutes the thoughts and images of the mind. The horse, the dog, and the camel that arise in the mind are not made of anything material; they are made of Consciousness. The aphorism says that the mind-stuff that forms itself into a camel, a dog, or a horse is nothing but a pulsation of the same Consciousness that has formed the universe. Another aphorism in the *Pratyabhijñā-hṛdayam* is: "By the power of Her own will alone, She unfolds the universe upon Her own screen,"[17] which means that Consciousness, that divine energy, has created the universe out of its own being, without taking the help of anything outside itself. In the same way, when Consciousness becomes the mind by assuming limitations, it begins to create endless mental universes. There are many outer universes, but they are all contained in Consciousness. In the same way, the universes that vibrate in the mind should not be seen as different from Consciousness. If you can look at your mind in this way, you will have very good meditation.

Let your mind spin as much as it wants to; do not try to subdue it. Simply witness the different thoughts as they arise and subside. No matter what thoughts and images arise in the mind, be aware that there is no concrete material from which they are being manifested. They are simply a phantasmagoria of Consciousness, and no matter how many worlds of desires, wishes, and positive and negative thoughts your mind creates, you should realize that they are all a play of Consciousness. When thoughts or images arise in your meditation, maintain the awareness of equality—the understanding that all objects are nothing but different forms of the Self. Be aware that even the worst thought is God. This understanding is vital to meditation. Your goal is not to battle with the mind, but to witness the mind. Know that you are the witness, the Self, and let the mind go wherever it likes. If you meditate with this awareness—that whatever is, is God—your mind will become calm very soon, and that will be high meditation.

MANTRA

ANOTHER GREAT MEANS of dealing with the mind is to take the support of the mantra. In India, there is a saying that the best way to take a thorn out of one's foot is with another thorn. In the same way, according to the scriptures, when one wants to still the mind, which revels in thoughts, one takes the help of one thought: the mantra.

The word *mantra* means that which redeems and protects the one who contemplates it. Mantra is the very life of meditation, the greatest of all techniques. A mantra is a cosmic word or sound vibration. It is the vibration of the Self, the true speech of the Self, and when we immerse ourselves in it, it leads us to the place of the Self.

Mantras consist of letters, which form words, which form sentences, which take us to their goal. Whether in mundane or spiritual life, all our work is carried out through mantras, through words. Without words, we cannot communicate with one another.

Mantras bear their fruit very quickly. The great saint Tukārām said: "When the name of God is on the tongue, liberation is in your hand." This should not be surprising, because in mundane life we use words, and they bear fruit immediately. I can make you happy immediately by using a few sweet words, by praising you and saying how beautiful you are. I can also make you agitated by using a few abusive words, by saying how bad you are.

Once a saint was giving a lecture on mantra. He was saying, "Mantra is great. Mantra takes us to God." Someone shouted from the back of the room, "How can you say that a mantra takes us to God? If I say, 'Bread, bread, bread,' will that get me bread?"

"Sit down, you bastard!" the saint shouted.

When the man heard this, he became furious. He began to shake and his hair stood on end. Even his necktie began to vibrate. He shouted, "You call yourself a saint, and yet you use such a filthy word for me?"

"I'm sorry, sir," the saint said. "Please, be calm and tell me what happened."

"You have the audacity to ask me what happened! Don't you realize how you have insulted me?"

"I used just one abusive word," the saint said, "and it has had such a powerful effect on you! When this is the case with an abusive term, what makes you think that the name of God, which is the supreme Truth, does not have its own power and will not also affect you?" If abusive words can make our blood boil, how can the name of God not have the power to change us?

Mantra has the greatest power. The sages of India, through the power of mantra, could burn whole mountains without fire. Through the power of mantra, they could bring entire universes into existence.

The scriptures say: *mantraḥ maheśvaraḥ,* "Mantra is God." There is no difference between God and his name; mantra has all the power of God. In the *Gītā,* the Lord says: *mantro'ham,* "[In all rituals] I am the mantra."[18] As we repeat the mantra, we should focus our attention within, on the place that is the source of the mantra. As we repeat the mantra more and more, it penetrates the entire territory of our mind, our intellect, and our imagination, and purifies it completely.

It is very important to repeat the mantra with the understanding of its meaning. Moreover, one who wants to attain the power of mantra, who wants to merge into mantra, should have the awareness that the goal of the mantra is one's own Self, that there is no difference between oneself, the mantra, and the goal of the mantra. If we hear an abusive word, we immediately identify ourselves as the object of that word, and that is why it has such an effect on us.

The only reason that a mantra does not affect us as profoundly as an abusive word is that we do not identify with it in the same way. If a person keeps himself, the mantra, and the goal of the mantra separate, he will never realize the goal of the mantra. Kashmir Shaivism says that we should meditate on God by becoming God; only then can we attain God.

There are eighty-four million mantras that can be found in books or obtained from different teachers. However, a mantra is not truly effective unless it is a conscious mantra, an enlivened mantra. A conscious mantra is one that has been received from a Guru who received it from his own Guru, repeated it himself, and attained full realization of his own inner Self. Such a mantra has the full power of the Guru's realization behind it, and when we repeat it in meditation, our meditation becomes infused with the force of that realization.

The power that flows through such a Self-realized Guru is the grace-bestowing power of the Supreme, and that same power exists in his mantra. Traditionally, a Guru initiates a disciple through a mantra, and mantra is one of the means through which the Guru gives *śaktipāt.* As we repeat the mantra with great love and reverence during meditation, it begins to work within. The energy of the Guru's conscious mantra, which is the energy of the supreme Guru, enters us and awakens our own inner energy, our own *śakti.*

ĀSANA

ANOTHER IMPORTANT FACTOR in meditation is the sitting posture, or *āsana.* The sitting posture is the foundation on which the whole structure of yoga rests. The *Yoga-sūtra* says that the correct sitting posture is that in which one can sit comfortably for a long time.[19] For meditation, the most important thing in *āsana* is that the spine be kept straight. If the back is kept straight, the mind becomes steady in the heart.

There are three sitting postures that are suitable for meditation; however, if one is too uncomfortable sitting, one can stretch out on the back in *śavāsana,* the corpse pose, and meditate in that position. The three main postures are *padmāsana,* the lotus posture; *siddhāsana,* the perfect posture;

and *sukhāsana,* the easy posture. Everyone must be familiar with the lotus posture, in which the legs are folded one over the other. The lotus posture is particularly important because if one sits in this position for one and one-half hours, it will completely purify the seventy-two million *nāḍīs,* or inner subtle channels. If you cannot sit in the lotus posture, sit in the easy posture, with one leg folded over the other. If you keep sitting in either of these postures steadily, the mind will begin to turn inward, and meditation will happen on its own. When you keep moving the body continually, the mind becomes restless. As the posture becomes steady, the *prāṇa* automatically becomes steady. As the *prāṇa* becomes steady, the mind becomes steady; and as the mind becomes steady, you begin to drink the joy that is in the heart.

PRĀṆĀYĀMA

THE FINAL FACTOR IN MEDITATION is *prāṇāyāma,* the breathing process. People practice many different kinds of *prāṇāyāma.* Some people practice it so much that they ruin their minds, their intellects, and their bodies. In meditation, the breathing process should be natural and spontaneous. We should not try to disturb the natural rhythm of the breath.

The mind and the *prāṇa* work in conjunction with each other. So let the rhythm of your breathing be natural. As you repeat the mantra, the breath will go in and out in time with the rhythm of the mantra and will become steady by itself.

THE PROCESS OF MEDITATION

THERE ARE FOUR FACTORS INVOLVED in meditation: the object of meditation, which is the inner Self; mantra, which is the vibration of the Self; *āsana,* the posture in which we can sit comfortably for a long time; and natural *prāṇāyāma,* which arises when we repeat the mantra with love and reverence. These four factors are interrelated, and when they come together, meditation occurs in a very natural manner.

Meditation on the Self is very easy. All that we really need are love and interest. As we meditate more and more, the inner *śakti* awakens and begins to unfold. The more intensely we long for meditation, the more we long for God, the more desire we have for the inner awakening, the closer we come to it. And the more we honor the *śakti,* the more we revere and worship it, the more actively it works inside us. When three factors come together — our faith in the *śakti,* the *śakti,* and the Guru, who is the activator of the *śakti* — there is an explosion of meditation within. Just as the *śakti* creates universes in the outer world, when it begins to work inside us, it creates a new inner universe, a universe of unending enthusiasm, a universe of supreme bliss.

The inner universe is much greater than the outer universe; it is so vast that the entire outer cosmos can be kept in just one corner of it. Everything is contained within it, and that is why, in meditation, the Indian seers were able to discover all the secrets of the universe.

Within us are infinite miracles, infinite wonders. As we go deeper into meditation, we come to understand the reality of all the different inner worlds we read about in the scriptures. Within these inner spaces, nectarean music resounds—all the different musical instruments were originally made by yogis after they had listened to this inner music. Within us are such delicious nectars that nothing in this world can compare with them in sweetness. There are suns so effulgent that the outer sun looks dull beside them. We should meditate systematically and with great persistence and go deeper and deeper within the body. In this way, meditation will be a gradual unfolding of our inner being.

Along the way will be many experiences, and these experiences are fine. However, the true state is beyond them. As we go deeper into meditation, we reach a place where we see nothing and hear nothing. Here there is nothing but bliss. This is the place of the Self, and true meditation is to become immersed in That.

The seers of Vedānta explained that our spirit is encased not just in one body, but in four, and that as we meditate, we pass through each of these four bodies to the Truth that lies within them. The first is the physical body, in which we experience the waking state. This is the state in which we identify ourselves as the body. When we are in the waking state, if the body is experiencing pain and pleasure, we say, "I am experiencing pain" or "I am experiencing pleasure." As the *śakti* begins to work in this body, we may experience physical movements, called *kriyās,* that are part of the process of purification of the physical body. In meditation, when the meditator is in the gross state, he can see the physical body as a red light that surrounds him like a flame of fire. This light is the size of the body, and within it one can see many marvelous things. Sometimes one can even see the vital force and the different fluids circulating within the body.

As meditation deepens, the meditator passes from the gross body to the subtle body, which one can see as a white light. This light dwells in the throat center and is the size of the thumb. One experiences dreams in the subtle body; in this state, one becomes aware that one is different from the physical body.

As the meditator goes deeper, he passes from the white, thumb-sized light to the light of the third body, which is black and the size of a fingertip. This is the causal body, the body of deep sleep. It is the state of total darkness, of total oblivion. In this state, the small self retires into the universal Self, and one is not even conscious of who or what one is. In this state, one experiences great peace. This is the state of the void.

However, if a seeker has deep love for the Guru and has deep faith in his grace and in Kuṇḍalinī, he passes from the third plane to the fourth plane, the state of *turīya,* the transcendent state. Then he sees the tiny blue light, the light of the Self, which we call the Blue Pearl.

The Blue Pearl is the most intimate body of the soul, and it is fascinatingly beautiful. As meditation deepens, one begins to see it sparkling and scintillating in the topmost spiritual center, the *sahasrāra.* The Blue Pearl is the vehicle of the individual soul. It is in the Blue Pearl that the soul leaves the body after death and travels to different worlds. It is extremely fine and subtle, and it moves like lightning. Sometimes it comes out of the meditator's eyes and stands in front of him, moving so subtly that the eyes do not feel its passage.

The Blue Pearl is the size of a sesame seed, but in reality it is so vast that it contains the entire universe. We are able to function because of the dynamism of the Blue Pearl. Because of its presence, the breath moves in and out of our bodies. The rays of its divine love keep flowing through us, and because of these rays we feel love for each other. The light of the Blue Pearl lights up our faces and our hearts; it is because of this light that we give love to others. If this light left the body, the body would have no radiance and no attraction. It would be of no use to anyone, and it would have to be discarded. The Blue Pearl is the abode of God, the form of the Self within us. Once you begin to see it in yourself, you will also begin to see it in others. As you continue to meditate, one day this light will expand, and within it you will see the entire cosmos. As you become immersed in this light, you will know, "I am God. I am Brahman." It was after having this experience that the Sūfī saint Mansūr Mastānā said, "Whatever I see around me is nothing but an expansion of my own being. I am not this body. I am the light that spreads everywhere."

This state is the culmination of meditation. In this state, our limitations vanish; our sense of individuality melts away. We attain divine vision, so that we no longer see this world as filled with duality and diversity. Instead of seeing differences between man and woman, East and West, past and future, we understand this whole universe as an expansion of our own Self. We realize that everything is a play of Consciousness and that just as the bubbles and waves of the ocean arise and subside in the ocean, whatever exists arises and subsides in the Self.

It is to attain this state that one should meditate, that one's *śakti* should be awakened. After one has reached this state, one no longer has to close one's eyes and sit for meditation; meditation goes on all the time. During formal meditation one experiences the highest bliss, but even in the waking state one experiences the joy of *samādhi,* seeing the entire waking world as an expansion of the same Consciousness. Wherever one looks, one sees God. Whatever one hears, one hears God. This is known as the state of natural *samādhi,* the state of the great beings, and in this state one continuously drinks the bliss that is in the heart.

SIDDHA MEDITATION

IF WE ARE GOING TO REALIZE this state of oneness at the end of our practice of meditation, why should we not understand it at the beginning and practice meditation with the awareness that everything is Śiva? This is how the great beings meditate, and if we also learn to see with this awareness, our meditation will be great. To meditate in this way, we do not have to undergo any difficulties. We do not have to make the mind still. We do not even have to close our eyes. Utpaladeva, the great sage and philosopher of Kashmir Shaivism, says: "One who is constantly aware that this entire universe is his own glory retains his divinity even if thoughts and fancies play in his mind."[20]

Truly speaking, everything is Consciousness. It is only because of our sense of limited individuality that we see things differently. A man is Consciousness, a woman is Consciousness, a dog is Consciousness, a donkey is Consciousness, a stone is Consciousness, and a mountain is Consciousness. This is true understanding. This is the knowledge we obtain through meditation, and the moment we obtain this knowledge, we begin to understand everything as it is.

In order to rid yourself of the feeling of limitation and obtain this understanding, you should practice the *sādhanā* of Śiva. You should understand, "I am Śiva—God. It is God who is meditating, and all the objects of my meditation are God. My *sādhanā* is God, and everybody and everything I see is God." For a long time, you have had the awareness, "I am an individual being, I am small, I am limited." This is why it is difficult for you to accept immediately the awareness, "I am God." All your life, you have been hearing that you are a sinner. Your teachers, all the holy books, and people pursuing different religious paths have been telling you that you are a sinner, and you have come to believe it. In this way, you impose the idea of sin onto the Self, which is totally pure and free of sin. It is because one has this wrong understanding that one identifies oneself with the wrong things. That is why one cannot uplift oneself; that is why one cannot have faith in the Self or become one-pointed on the Self. Kashmir Shaivism teaches that when one begins to think, "I am this, I am that, I am a sinner, I am an inferior person," one becomes poor in *śakti,* and that is how one becomes an individual being.

In Vedānta, this is often explained by a story. One day, a washerman took several donkeys to a forest to graze them. There he came upon a lion cub; he did not know that it was a lion, and he brought it home with him. The lion cub grew up with the donkeys. Living in their company, he began to repeat the donkey mantra, *hee-haw, hee-haw,* to eat with them, and to travel back and forth to the river, carrying filthy laundry. As the lion grew up, he thought of himself as a donkey and shared the donkeys' habits and their ways.

One day when he was grazing on the river bank with his donkey brothers, another lion came along to drink from the river. While this lion was drinking, he suddenly caught sight of the young lion in the midst of the donkeys. The old lion was shocked to see his brother in such a pitiful condition. He moved closer to him and said, "Brother, what are you up to?"

"I am with my brothers," said the young lion.

"How can you call them brothers? They are asses and you are a lion. Come with me and look at your reflection in the water. Look at your reflection and my reflection, and see if there is anything similar about us."

The young lion gazed down at his reflection and saw that he looked just like the old lion.

"Are they your brothers or am I your brother? Now stop going *hee-haw* and start roaring!"

The young lion began to roar, and all the donkeys ran away.

The two lions ran into the forest. The young lion had been transformed from a donkey to a lion; he had become free.

Actually, the lion cub had never been a donkey. He had only thought he was a donkey, and this is exactly the situation we are in. We are not donkeys. We are not limited, imperfect beings. We are not sinners. We never became small; we only believe we are small. So we must discard this belief and become aware of our own strength. Kashmir Shaivism says that when *citi,* universal Consciousness, accepts limitations, it begins to believe itself to be bound. Just as *citi* becomes smaller and smaller by descending from its status as pure Consciousness and becomes a limited individual soul, when it reverses the process, it can become greater and greater and regain its original nature. It is only our awareness that has to be changed. We never became donkeys and we never can become donkeys because we are the pure Self.

To rid yourself of wrong understanding, you do not have to do anything new. All you have to do is meditate. The fact is that you meditate not to attain God, but to become aware that God is within you. Kashmir Shaivism says: *nāśivam vidyate kvacit,* "Nothing exists that is not Śiva."[21] Where is that place where there is no Śiva? Where is that time where there is no Śiva? So even if you experience duality, even if you see diversity around you, consider yourself to be Śiva. Understand that it is Śiva who is eating, Śiva who is the food that is eaten, Śiva who gives, and Śiva who takes. It is Śiva who does everything. The entire universe is the glory of Śiva, the glory of the Self.

MEDITATION INSTRUCTIONS

Preparing for Meditation

IT IS VERY GOOD TO SET ASIDE a place for meditation. If possible, have a special room, but if not, a corner will do. Purify it by chanting God's name, and try not to let anything take place there that will disturb its atmosphere. In the place where you meditate regularly, the vibrations of meditation gather, and after a while it becomes very easy to meditate there. For the same reason, you should set aside special clothes and a mat for meditation; do not wash them too often, because the *śakti* will accumulate in them and make it easy for you to meditate.

If possible, meditate at the same time every day. The early hours of the morning, between three and six, are the best for meditation, but you can meditate at any time that is convenient. If you become accustomed to meditating at a certain hour, your body will develop the habit of meditation. I have been meditating every morning at three o'clock for many years, and even now my body automatically goes into meditation at that hour.

The Attitude of Meditation

JUST AS YOU SLIP EASILY into sleep, you should be able to slip easily into meditation. Sit peacefully; be with yourself. Focus your mind on the inner Consciousness, the inner knower. Let your breath move naturally and watch it; do not force anything. Become immersed in your own inner Self. Turn your mind and senses inward. Absorb yourself in the pure "I."

If thoughts arise, let them come and go. Watch the source of your thoughts. Meditate with the awareness that you are the witness of the mind. True meditation is to become free from mentation. The moment the thoughts become still, the light of the Self will shine from within. However, if the mind does not immediately become thought-free, do not try to erase the thoughts forcibly. Respect the mind, understanding that whatever comes and goes within it is a form of the Self. Then it will become still on its own.

To help in stilling the mind, you may take the support of the mantra. Repeat either *Oṁ Namaḥ Śivāya* or *So'ham*. Both mantras are one; both come from the Self. Only the method of repeating them differs.

Oṁ Namaḥ Śivāya

OṀ NAMAḤ ŚIVĀYA MEANS, "I bow to the Lord, who is the inner Self." Repeat it silently, at the same rate of speed with which you speak. Repeat it with love, and go deep inside. Understand that you yourself are the deity of the mantra. Listen to it. When every letter pulsates in your mind, try to experience it.

Lose yourself in meditation. No matter what feeling arises, let it be. Do not fear. The inner energy is filled with infinite techniques, processes, and feelings. Its play is in everything. Therefore, everything belongs to it, and it is one with your Self.

The purpose of meditation is inner happiness, inner peace. It is fine to have visions, but they are not absolutely necessary. What is necessary is inner joy. When all the senses become quiet and you experience bliss, that is the attainment. The world is the embodiment of joy; joy lies everywhere. Find it and attain it. Instead of having negative thoughts, have the awareness, "I am pure, I am joy." Feel good about yourself; fill yourself with great divinity.

Meditate with this understanding: "Neither am I different from God, nor is God different from me." Then not only will you attain God, but you yourself will become God.

Become quiet with the awareness that everything is you and you are everything.

Meditate on your Self. Honor your Self. Understand your Self. God dwells within you as you.

Your own,

Swami Muktānanda

Guide to Sanskrit Pronunciation

In Sanskrit every letter is pronounced; there are no silent letters. Every letter has only one sound, except for the letter **v** (see below).

LENGTH OF VOWELS

Vowels are either short or long. Short vowels are **a**, **i**, **u**, and **ṛ**. Long vowels are **ā**, **ī**, **ū**, **e**, and **o**. A long vowel is held for twice as long as a short one.

VOWELS

The English equivalents are approximations.

a	as in *but* or *cup*	**ā**	as in *father* or *calm*
i	as in *sit* or *pick*	**ī**	as in *seat* or *clean*
u	as in *put* or *pull*	**ū**	as in *pool* or *mood*
e	as in *save* or *wait*	**o**	as in *coat* or *cone*

ṛ is a vowel pronounced with the tip of the tongue bent slightly back toward the roof of the mouth, while making a sound between the **ur** in *curd* and the **ri** in *cricket*.

The next two vowels are diphthongs, combinations of sounds that are made up of two distinct vowels pronounced in rapid succession. Each diphthong, represented by two letters in transliteration, is written as a single letter in the Sanskrit alphabet and has the same length as a long vowel.

ai as in *pie* or *sky*

au as in *town* or *cow*

CONSONANTS

c	as in *such,* never as in *cave* or *celery*
s	as in *seek* or *sight*
ś	as in *shine* or *shower*
ṣ	is pronounced like **ś**, except that the tip of the tongue is bent slightly back toward the roof of the mouth, as in English *assure.*
t, d, n	are pronounced with the tip of the tongue against the top teeth.
ṭ, ḍ, ṇ	are pronounced with the tip of the tongue bent slightly back to touch the roof of the mouth.
ph	as in *pin* or *u**p**hold,* never as in ***ph**oto* or ***ph**ase*
th	as in *top* or *ho**th**ouse,* never as in ***th**ink* or ***th**ere*
ṁ	denotes not the consonant *m,* but simply a nasalization of the preceding vowel, as in the three nasal sounds in the French phrase ***un** gr**an**d p**on**t.*
ṅ	as in *i**n**k, i**n**got,* or *si**ng***
ñ	as in *be**n**ch* or *e**n**joy*
jñ	as **gny**. Represents a single letter in the Sanskrit alphabet.
r	is a rolled **r**, as in Spanish *para.*
v	is a soft **v** when following a vowel or beginning a word; when following a consonant (as in *tvam*), it is like a **w** but with minimal rounding of the lips.
ḥ	at the end of a line, indicates that the previous vowel (or the second vowel in a preceding diphthong) is echoed; for example, *śāntiḥ* is pronounced *śānti**hi**,* and durjayaiḥ as durjayai***hi.***

When consonants are followed by **h**, as in **bh**, **ph**, **dh**, **gh**, or **ch**, the consonant is aspirated, as in *a**bh**or, u**ph**old, a**dh**ere, do**gh**ouse* or *woo**dch**uck.*

A consonant written twice, such as **dd** or **tt**, is pronounced as a single sound and is held twice as long as a single consonant.

Notes

FOREWORD

1. *Meditate: Happiness Lies Within You,* 1.
2. *Viveka-cūḍāmaṇi,* 132
3. Saint Teresa of Ávila, in *The Complete Works of Saint Teresa of Jesus,* E. Allison Peers, trans. and ed. (London: Sheed and Ward, 1946), vol. 1, 180.
4. *Meditate: Happiness Lies Within You,* 37.
5. Ibid., 10.
6. Ibid., 16.
7. *Maitrī Upaniṣad,* 6.34
8. *Meditate: Happiness Lies Within You,* 27.

TEXT

1. *Bhagavad-gītā* 13.2
2. *Bhagavad-gītā* 13.3
3. *Ātmabodha* 36, echoing *Bṛhad-āraṇyaka Upaniṣad* 1.4.10
4. *Bṛhaj-jābāla Upaniṣad* 8.6
5. Kṣemarāja, *Pratyabhijñā-hṛdayam* 1
6. *Knowledge* refers here to the direct experience in which the Self knows itself, without the aid of the senses, mind, or intellect.

7. *Yoga-vāsiṣṭha*
8. Śiva, in this connection, refers not to the Hindu deity, but to the all-pervasive Consciousness, or God, of which Śiva is one name.
9. Abhinavagupta, *Tantrasāra* 2.6: "The net of *sādhanā* cannot reveal Śiva. Can a clay pot illuminate the conscious sun?"
10. Patañjali, *Yoga-sūtra*, 1.2 and 1.3
11. *Yoga-sūtra* 3.1
12. Sundardās, "*jo man nārī kī or nihārat,*" a devotional song (*bhajan*) originally in Hindi.
13. *Bṛhad-āraṇyaka Upaniṣad* 3.7.20
14. *Kena Upaniṣad* 1.5
15. *Bhagavad-gītā* 13.15
16. *Pratyabhijñā-hṛdayam* 5
17. *Pratyabhijñā-hṛdayam* 2
18. *Bhagavad-gītā* 9.16
19. *Yoga-sūtra* 2.46
20. *Īśvara-pratyabhijñā* 4.12
21. *Svacchanda-tantra* 4.314

Glossary

All non-English terms are Sanskrit unless otherwise indicated.

ABSOLUTE (Sanskrit: Brahman)
The highest Reality; supreme Consciousness; the pure, untainted, changeless Truth. *See also* CONSCIOUSNESS.

AHAṀ BRAHMĀSMI
One of the four great statements (*mahā-vākyas*) of Vedānta. It means, "I am Brahman," the supreme Absolute. *See also* ABSOLUTE; VEDĀNTA.

ĀNANDA
Divine bliss; unbounded, transcendent, independent happiness.

APĀNA
One of the five types of *prāṇa*; specifically, the downward-moving life force that governs the expulsion of air and the excretion of wastes from the body. *See also* PRĀṆA.

ARJUNA
One of the warrior heroes from the Indian epic *Mahābhārata*; a disciple of Lord Kṛṣṇa. It was to Arjuna that Kṛṣṇa imparted his teachings in the *Bhagavad-gītā*. *See also* BHAGAVAD-GĪTĀ; KṚṢṆA.

ĀSANA
A *haṭha-yoga* posture, practiced to strengthen and purify the body and develop one-pointedness of mind; a posture for meditation; also, a seat or mat on which one sits for meditation. *See also* YOGA.

ASHRAM (Hindi: *āśram*; Sanskrit: *āśrama*)
A place of disciplined retreat, where seekers engage in spiritual practice and study sacred teachings.

ĀTMAN
See SELF.

BHAGAVAD-GĪTĀ
Lit., "song of the Lord." One of the world's treasures of spiritual

wisdom, the centerpiece of the Indian epic *Mahābhārata.* In its eighteen chapters, Lord Kṛṣṇa instructs his disciple Arjuna about steady wisdom, meditation, the nature of God, the supreme Self, and spiritual knowledge and practice. *See also* KṚṢṆA; SELF.

BISTĀMĪ, HAZRAT BĀYAZĪD
An ecstatic ninth-century Sūfī saint of northeastern Persia, also known as Abū Yazīd al-Bistāmī; author of many poems that boldly portray the mystic's total absorption in God. *See also* SŪFĪ.

BLUE PEARL (Sanskrit: *nīla-bindu*)
The point of pure Consciousness within each individual that is the core of our true identity and the source of all our powers of perception and action. It is depicted as shining in the space in the crown of the head; a vision of the Blue Pearl is considered to be an auspicious glimpse of the innermost Self. *See also* CONSCIOUSNESS; SELF.

BRAHMAN
See ABSOLUTE.

BṚHAJ-JĀBĀLA UPANIṢAD
A minor Upaniṣad, appended to the *Atharva-veda,* which expounds the divinity of Kālāgni Rudra, a form of Lord Śiva, as well as various forms of yogic practice. *See also* ŚIVA; UPANIṢAD(S); YOGA.

CAKRA
Lit., "wheel." A subtle energy center in the body; a nexus point of subtle energy channels (*nāḍīs*) through which Kuṇḍalinī passes on her journey as she moves through the central energy channel (*suṣumnā nāḍī*). The subtle body is depicted as having seven lotus-like *cakras,* extending from the *mūlādhāra* at the base of the spine to the *sahasrāra* in the crown of the head. *See also* KUṆḌALINĪ.

CITI (fem.; masc. = *cit*)
Lit., "Consciousness." The all-pervasive dynamic power of supreme Consciousness that creates, sustains, and dissolves the entire universe; also, the power that conceals and reveals the Truth in human beings. *When capitalized*: The personification of this power as the Goddess, and sometimes more specifically as Kuṇḍalinī, the power of spiritual evolution in a human being. *See also* CONSCIOUSNESS; TRUTH.

CONSCIOUSNESS (Sanskrit: *cit, citi*)
When capitalized: The luminous, self-aware, and creative Reality that is the essential Self of all that exists; a name for God, the Absolute, the supreme Truth. *See also* SELF.

DHĀRAṆĀ
A centering technique or spiritual exercise in which holding a steady inner focus intensifies one's awareness, with the goal of connecting with the Heart, the divine Self. *See also* SELF.

EGO (Sanskrit: *ahaṅkāra*, lit., "I-maker")
A faculty of the mind which, in Indian philosophy, constructs one's sense of limited identity, creates the illusion of a separate self with a specific personality and qualities, and appropriates specific objects and experiences to itself. The limitations of the ego can be transcended by engaging in the spiritual practices of *sādhanā*. *See also* SĀDHANĀ.

GĪTĀ
See BHAGAVAD-GĪTĀ.

GURU
Lit., "a venerable person, a spiritual preceptor, a teacher." *When capitalized:* A realized Master, a true Guru. *See also* SIDDHA GURU.

HAṬHA-YOGA
The yogic practice of physical postures and breathing techniques for the purpose of strengthening the body and stilling the mind. *See also* YOGA.

INITIATION (Sanskrit: *dīkṣā*)
A rite of passage by which a novice is introduced to a particular tradition or practice. In Siddha Yoga, initiation (*dīkṣā*) takes the form of the awakening of the seeker's Kuṇḍalinī energy by the grace of the Siddha Guru; this initiation is known as *śaktipāt dīkṣā*. *See also* KUṆḌALINĪ; ŚAKTIPĀT; SIDDHA GURU.

KASHMIR SHAIVISM
The nondual Shaivism of medieval Kashmir, a philosophy elaborated in the collective writings of a number of sages from Kashmir for whom the name Śiva denoted the ultimate Reality. These sages, who flourished from the ninth through the twelfth centuries, recognized the

entire universe as a manifestation of Śiva's Śakti or divine power. Swami Muktānanda found his own experience reflected in the writings of these sages and incorporated many of their core teachings into the philosophical framework of the Siddha Yoga path. *See also* ŚAKTI; ŚIVA.

KENA UPANIṢAD
A principal Upaniṣad, which establishes that Brahman, the Absolute, is the supreme Reality, and the power which enables the mind, speech, and senses to perform their functions. *See also* UPANIṢAD(S).

KRIYĀ
Lit, "action; divine action." A physical, mental, or emotional process initiated by the awakened Kuṇḍalinī, which brings about higher states of meditation by purifying the *saṁskāras* (impressions left on the subtle body by past actions or experiences) that block the channels of the subtle body. *See also* KUṆḌALINĪ; SUBTLE BODY.

KṚṢṆA
Lit., "dark one." The eighth incarnation of Lord Viṣṇu (a name for the all-pervasive, supreme Reality, the sustainer of the universe), called Kṛṣṇa because of the blue-black color of his skin. *See also* BHAGAVAD-GĪTĀ.

KUṆḌALINĪ
Lit., "coiled one." The Goddess Kuṇḍalinī; also, the power of spiritual evolution in a human being. The dormant form of this spiritual energy is represented as lying coiled at the base of the spine; when awakened and guided by a Siddha Guru and nourished by the seeker's disciplined effort, this energy brings about purification of the seeker's being at all levels, and leads to the permanent experience of one's divine nature. *See also* ŚAKTIPĀT; SIDDHA GURU.

KUṆḌALINĪ ŚAKTI
See KUṆḌALINĪ.

LIBERATION (Sanskrit: *mokṣa*)
Freedom from the cycle of birth and death; the realization of one's own divine Self. *See also* SELF.

MAITRĪ UPANIṢAD

An Upaniṣad which focuses on the nature of the Self and on attaining the knowledge of the Self through meditation, austerity, and contemplation. *See also* SELF; UPANIṢAD(S).

MANTRA

A sacred invocation. Sacred words or divine sounds invested with the power to protect, purify, and transform the awareness of the individual who repeats them. A mantra received from an enlightened Master is enlivened by the power of the Master's attainment. *See also* OṀ NAMAḤ ŚIVĀYA.

MASTĀNĀ, MANSŪR

(852–922) A Persian Sūfī mystic who, having attained the ultimate state of meditation, saw everything around him as an expansion of his own being, declaring: *ana'l-haqq*, "I am God." *See also* SŪFĪ.

MASTER

See SIDDHA GURU.

MŪLĀDHĀRA-CAKRA

Lit., "root-support (*mūlādhāra*) wheel (*cakra*)." The spiritual center in the subtle body located at a point corresponding to the base of the spine in the physical body; the dwelling place of the coiled Kuṇḍalinī, or divine power, in her dormant form. *See also* KUṆḌALINĪ; SUBTLE BODY.

NĀḌĪ

A channel through which the life force is circulated in the human body. In the physical body, *nāḍīs* take the form of blood vessels, nerves, and lymph ducts; in the subtle body, they constitute a complex system of channels through which the *prāṇa* flows. *See also* PRĀṆĀ; SUBTLE BODY.

NASRUDDĪN, SHEIKH

A popular character in Turkish and Persian folklore, who is used as a central figure in teaching stories to illustrate spiritual lessons and the foibles of the human mind; also known as Mullāh Nasruddīn.

OṀ NAMAḤ ŚIVĀYA

The initiation mantra of the Siddha Yoga path, known as the great redeeming mantra for its power to grant both worldly fulfillment and spiritual realization. *Oṁ* is the primordial sound; *namaḥ* is an expression of reverence or honor; *śivāya* denotes "to Śiva" or "to divine Consciousness" (the Lord who dwells within). *See also* CONSCIOUSNESS; MANTRA; SIDDHA YOGA; ŚIVA.

PATAÑJALI
(ca. third century CE) Sage and author of the *Yoga-sūtra,* the authoritative text on one of the six orthodox philosophies of India. *See also* YOGA-SŪTRA(S).

PRĀṆA
The vital, life-sustaining force of all living things, linked to the breath. Also, the name given to one of the five types of *prāṇa*; the Shaivite scripture *Vijñāna Bhairava* uses *prāṇa* in this narrower sense to refer to the exhalation, whereas the Upaniṣads and certain yogic texts use it to refer to the inhalation. *See also* UPANIṢAD(S); VIJÑĀNA BHAIRAVA.

PRĀṆĀYĀMA
Lit., "restraining the breath." A yogic technique, consisting of systematic regulation and restraint of the breath, which leads to steadiness of mind. It may also occur spontaneously through the power of the awakened Kuṇḍalinī. *See also* KUṆḌALINĪ; YOGA.

PRATYABHIJÑĀ-HṚDAYAM
Lit., "the heart of recognition." An eleventh-century treatise by Kṣemarāja that expounds on the *pratyabhijñā* (recognition) philosophy of Kashmir Shaivism. It teaches that individuals, having forgotten their true nature, can once again recognize their own Self through divine grace and an experiential understanding of supreme Consciousness as the essence of all creation. *See also* CONSCIOUSNESS; KASHMIR SHAIVISM; SELF.

RĀMA (Hindi = Rām)
A name for God. Also, the legendary hero who was the seventh incarnation of Viṣṇu (a name for the all-pervasive, supreme Reality, the sustainer of the universe), the central character in the Indian epic *Rāmāyaṇa,* and an exemplar of *dharma,* or righteousness.

SĀDHANĀ

Leading straight to a goal; a means of accomplishing (something); spiritual practice; worship. The *sādhanā* of Siddha Yoga students, which begins with *śaktipāt* initiation, includes active, disciplined engagement with the essential Siddha Yoga practices of meditation, chanting, *sevā* (selfless service), and *dakṣiṇā* (offering of financial resources), along with focused study and contemplation of the Siddha Yoga teachings. The goal of Siddha Yoga *sādhanā* is the spiritual transformation that leads to liberation. *See also* LIBERATION; ŚAKTIPĀT; SIDDHA YOGA.

SAHASRĀRA

Lit., "one thousand spokes." The highest spiritual center of the subtle body and the destination of the awakened Kuṇḍalinī; located at the crown of the head, it is often visualized or represented as a lotus with one thousand petals. *See also* KUṆḌALINĪ; SUBTLE BODY.

ŚAKTI

Power, energy, strength. Also, a specific power or energy, such as a power embodied in a particular goddess or within an aspirant. *When capitalized*: The creative power of the divine Absolute, which animates and sustains all forms of creation; often personified as the Goddess, and sometimes more specifically as Kuṇḍalinī Śakti, the power of spiritual evolution in a human being. *See also* ABSOLUTE; KUṆḌALINĪ.

ŚAKTIPĀT (Hindi; Sanskrit: *śakti-pāta*)

Lit., "descent of power; descent of grace." In Siddha Yoga, the initiation (*dīkṣā*) by which a Siddha Guru transmits the divine grace that awakens Kuṇḍalinī Śakti, the inner spiritual energy in an aspirant; *śaktipāt dīkṣā* signals the beginning of Siddha Yoga *sādhanā*, which culminates in spiritual liberation. *See also* KUṆḌALINĪ; LIBERATION; SĀDHANĀ; SIDDHA GURU; SIDDHA YOGA.

SAMĀDHI

The practice of absorption in the object of meditation. Also, the final stage of that practice, in which the meditator is absorbed in the Self. See also SELF.

ŚAṄKARĀCĀRYA

A venerated sage of the eighth century, who formalized the Advaita (nondual) school of Vedānta. He established monastic orders in India that exist to this day, including the Sarasvatī order, to which the Siddha Yoga Swamis belong. *See also* SIDDHA YOGA; SWAMI; VEDĀNTA.

SAT

See TRUTH.

SELF (Sanskrit: *ātman*)

When capitalized: The pure Consciousness that is both the divine core of a human being and the essential nature of all things. *See also* CONSCIOUSNESS.

SELF-REALIZATION

See LIBERATION; SELF.

SIDDHA

A perfected, fully accomplished, Self-realized yogi; an enlightened yogi who lives in the state of unity consciousness; one whose experience of the Self is uninterrupted and whose identification with the ego has been dissolved. *See also* EGO; SELF; YOGI.

SIDDHA GURU

A perfected spiritual Master who has realized his or her oneness with God, and who is able both to bestow *śaktipāt* initiation and to guide seekers to spiritual liberation. Such a Guru is also required to be learned in the scriptures and to belong to a lineage of Masters. *See also* LIBERATION; ŚAKTIPĀT; SIDDHA.

SIDDHA YOGA

The spiritual path taught by Gurumayi Chidvilāsānanda and her Guru, Swami Muktānanda. The journey of the Siddha Yoga path begins with *śaktipāt dīkṣā* (spiritual initiation). Through the grace of the Siddha Yoga Master and the student's own steady disciplined effort, the journey culminates in the constant recognition of divinity within oneself and within the world. *See also* SĀDHANĀ; ŚAKTIPĀT.

ŚIVA

Lit., "auspicious." In nondual Shaivism, the transcendent, immanent, and all-pervasive Reality, the one source of all existence. Also, absolute Reality personified as the supreme Deity, Lord Śiva. *See also* KASHMIR SHAIVISM.

SO'HAM
Lit., "That (*so*) I am (*aham*)." The natural vibration of the Self, which seekers experience within through the Guru's grace, and by which they become aware of their identity with the supreme Self. Also, the mantra formed by the syllables *so* (or *saḥ*) and *ham*, repeated with the breath. Also known as the mantra *haṁsa*. *See also* MANTRA; SELF.

SUBTLE BODY (Sanskrit: *sūkṣma-śarīra*)
The body that is composed of a subtle form of *prāṇa* (vital energy), considered in traditional Indian philosophy to be distinct from the gross or physical body; and which contains the system of energy centers and channels through which Kuṇḍalinī Śakti moves. *See also* CAKRA; KUṆḌALINĪ.

SŪFĪ
A practitioner of Sufism, the mystical tradition of Islam characterized by ecstatic devotion to God.

SUNDARDĀS
(ca. 1596–1689) A poet-saint of Delhi, India, who wrote eloquently about the significance of the spiritual Master and the requirements of discipleship.

SWAMI
A monk in an Indian monastic order. Some swamis are teachers. The ten monastic orders to which most of the swamis of India belong were founded by the sage Śaṅkarācārya in the eighth century. *See also* ŚAṄKARĀCĀRYA.

THAT (Sanskrit: *tat*)
When capitalized: The supreme Self, the Absolute. *See also* ABSOLUTE; SELF.

TRUTH (Sanskrit: *sat, satya, tattva, paramārtha*)
When capitalized: The highest Reality.

TUKĀRĀM MAHĀRĀJ
(ca. 1608–1650) A poet-saint of Mahārāṣṭra, India, who earned his

livelihood as a village grocer. After receiving spiritual initiation in a dream, Tukārām wrote thousands of devotional songs (*abhangas*), many of which describe his spiritual experiences and the glory of the divine Name.

TURĪYA

Lit., "fourth." The fourth or transcendental state (beyond the waking, dream, and deep-sleep states), in which one is completely free of identification with the body and mind; the state of *samādhi*, or deep meditation.

UPANIṢAD(S)

Lit., "the sitting down near (a teacher)" or "secret doctrine." The group of scriptures that distill the esoteric teachings of the Vedas and are the basis for Vedantic philosophy. Most of the various Upaniṣads illuminate the essential teaching that the individual soul and the Absolute are one. *See also* ABSOLUTE; VEDĀNTA; VEDA(S).

UTPALADEVA

A tenth-century philosopher, theologian, and poet who was one of the foremost sages of nondual Kashmir Shaivism. *See also* KASHMIR SHAIVISM.

VASIṢṬHA

The legendary sage and Guru of Lord Rāma, who, in the *Yogavāsiṣṭha* scripture, answers Lord Rāma's questions on the nature of life, death, and human suffering by teaching that the world is as you see it and that illusion ceases when the mind is stilled. *See also* RĀMA.

VEDĀNTA

Lit. "end of the Vedas." One of the six orthodox schools of Indian philosophy; its dominant branch is Advaita ("nondual") Vedānta, which teaches that one supreme Principle of being-consciousness-bliss (*sac-cid-ānanda*) constitutes the whole of Reality, and that the world of multiplicity is ultimately illusory. *See also* UPANIṢAD(S).

VIJÑĀNA BHAIRAVA

Lit., "wisdom of Bhairava, wisdom of the Lord." An exposition of the path of yoga based on the principles of the nondual Shaivism of Kashmir. Originally composed in the ninth century, it is a compilation of 112 *dhāraṇās* (centering techniques), any of which can give the immediate experience of one's identity with the Divine. *See also* DHĀRAṆĀ; KASHMIR SHAIVISM; YOGA.

VIVEKA-CŪḌĀMIṆI

Lit., "the crest jewel of discrimination." A Sanskrit commentary by the eighth-century sage Śaṅkarācārya on Advaita (nondual) Vedānta, expounding the teaching that the Absolute alone is real. *See also* ABSOLUTE; ŚAṄKARĀCĀRYA; VEDĀNTA.

YOGA

Lit., "yoking; joining." A method or set of disciplined spiritual practices (including meditation, mantra repetition, concentration, posture, sense control, and ethical precepts) whose ultimate goal is the constant experience of union with the divine Self. *See also* MANTRA; SELF.

YOGA-SŪTRA(S)

(ca. third century CE) A collection of aphorisms, written by the sage Patañjali, that expounds a set of specific and practical methods for the attainment of the goal of yoga, or mental tranquility, in which the movement of the mind ceases and the Self rests in its own blissful nature as the witness of the mind. *See also* PATAÑJALI; SELF; YOGA.

YOGI (masc.; fem. = *yoginī*)

One who practices yoga. *See also* YOGA.

Index

Absolute, 4
Ahaṁ brahmāsmi ("I am the Absolute"), 4
Anger, 17, 19
Apāna (exhalation), 11
Arjuna, 3, 17
Āsana (posture), 25-26, 27
Attainment, spiritual, 13, 15, 31, 37
Attention, turned within, 5, 24
Awakening, spiritual, 10-12, 27, 31
  See also *Śaktipāt*
Awareness
  inner, 6-7
  mantra and, 24
  meditation and, 32, 34, 36, 37
  of Self, 3-4, 18, 21-22, 34
  of Śiva, 31-32

Bhagavad-gītā, 3, 17, 24
Bistāmī, Hazrat Bāyazīd, 7-10
Bliss
  absolute, 14
  Consciousness and, 4
  meditation and, 10, 28, 31, 37
  śakti and, 27
  sleep and, 2
  See also Happiness
Blue Pearl, 29-30
Bodies, four, 28-29
Body, 3, 6, 10-11, 26, 28-30, 35
Books, 4
Breath, 11, 26, 30, 35
Bṛhaj-jābāla Upaniṣad, 10

Cakras, 11, 16
Chanting, 35
Citi (Consciousness), 10, 20, 34
Clothing, for meditation, 35
Concentration, 5, 16
Consciousness, 10, 13-14
  all-pervasiveness of, 31-32
  contraction of, 20-21
  creation and, 11
  experience of, 8
  limitation of, 34
  meditation and, 35
  mind and, 20-21
  Self and, 4
Contentment, 2

Death, 10, 30
Delusion, 6
Dhāraṇā (concentration), 16
Disease, 5-6
Divinity, 2-3, 7-10, 32, 37
Dreams, 3, 6-7, 29
Duality, 30-31, 34

Ego, 17
Elements, 5
Enthusiasm, 27
Equality consciousness, 21-22
Experience
  of happiness, 1-2
  in meditation, 6, 28
  of Self, 4, 11-13, 15, 16-17

Faith, 27, 29, 32
Fantasies, 17
Fear, 36
Field, knower of, 3
Focus, 5, 16, 19, 24, 35

God
  all-pervasiveness of, 14, 31-32
  Blue Pearl and, 30
  experience of, 7-10, 12-13, 15
  longing for, 27
  mantra and, 23-24
  meditation and, 4, 16, 32, 34, 37
  mind and, 17-18
  name of, 22-23, 35
  thoughts and, 22
Grace, 25, 29
Guru
  concentration on, 16
  love for, 29
  mantra and, 24-25
  meditation and, 27
  śaktipāt and, 10, 12
  Swami Muktānanda's, 4

Happiness, 1-2, 4, 26, 31, 37
  See also Bliss
Hazrat Bāyazīd Bistāmī, 7-10
Heart
  bliss of, 31
  Blue Pearl and, 30
  God and, 12-13
  meditation and, 2
  posture and, 25-26
  Self and, 4

I-Consciousness, pure, 3-4, 18, 36
Identification, with body, 28
Individuality, 30, 32, 33
  See also Soul, individual
Initiation, mantra and, 25
  See also *Śaktipāt*
Intellect, 14, 24, 26

Joy
  See Happiness

Kashmir Shaivism
  on creation, 11
  on limitation, 33-34
  on meditation, 24
  on *sādhanā*, 15
  on Śiva, 34
  on true attainment, 12-13
  on unity consciousness, 32
Kena Upaniṣad, 17
Knowledge, 4, 12-14, 15, 18, 32
Kṛṣṇa, Lord, 3, 17
Kriyās (movements), 28
Kuṇḍalinī, 10-11, 29

Liberation, 10, 23
  See also Self-realization
Light, 12-14, 29, 30, 36
Limitation, 20-21, 30, 32, 34
Logic, 4
Longing, for God, 27
Lotus posture, 25-26
Love, 2, 14, 27, 29, 30, 36

Mansūr Mastānā, 30
Mantra, 22-26, 27, 36
Master
  See Guru
Mat, for meditation, 35
Meditation
  breathing process and, 26
  culmination of, 30-31
  God and, 17-18, 24, 34
  happiness and, 2

Meditation (*continued*)
- mantra and, 22, 25
- mind and, 6, 18-22
- posture and, 25-26
- preparing for, 35
- process of, 27-31, 35-37
- Self and, 4, 7-10, 16-18, 27-28
- *śaktipāt* and, 12
- unity and, 31-32
- universality of, 5

Mind
- God and, 17-18
- knowledge and, 4
- mantra and, 22, 24
- meditation and, 6, 16, 18-22, 31, 35-36
- posture and, 25-26
- *prāṇa* and, 26
- Self and, 14, 16-17

Music, inner, 28

Nāḍīs (subtle channels), 26
Nasruddīn, Sheikh, 15
Nectar, 2, 28
Nityānanda, Bhagavān, 4

Oṁ Namaḥ Śivāya, 36

Padmāsana (lotus posture), 25-26
Pain and pleasure, 6-7, 14, 28
Patañjali, 16
Peace, 2, 4, 6, 29, 35, 37
Posture, sitting, 25-26, 27
Prāṇa (life force), 11, 26
Prāṇāyāma (breathing process), 26, 27
Practices, spiritual, 15
Pratyabhijñā-hṛdayam, 11, 20, 21
Purification, 5, 24, 28, 35

Rāma, Lord, 13
Repetition of mantra, 24, 25, 36

Sādhanā, 15, 32
Sages, 5, 23-24
Sahasrāra (crown chakra), 29
Śakti, 10, 35
- awakening of, 11, 12, 31
- in the body, 28
- mantra and, 25
- meditation and, 27
- poverty of, 33

Śaktipāt, 10-12, 25
Samādhi (meditative union), 31
Śaṅkarācārya, 4
Sat, cit, ānanda (existence, Consciousness, bliss), 13-14
Śavāsana (corpse pose), 25
Self
- all-pervasiveness of, 31
- awareness of, 21-22, 34
- Blue Pearl and, 30
- body and, 6
- experience of, 7-10, 11-15
- faith in, 32-33
- focus and, 5, 19
- four bodies and, 29
- happiness and, 1
- mantra and, 22, 24, 27
- meditation and, 4, 16-18, 27-28, 36, 37
- mind and, 16-17, 20
- nature of, 3-4
- purity of, 32

Self-realization, 4, 25
- *See also* Liberation

Senses, 1-2, 14, 17-18, 36, 37
Siddhāsana (perfect posture), 25
Śiva, 13, 31-32, 34
Sleep, 2, 3, 29, 35

So'ham, 36
Soul, individual, 29, 34
Stillness, 18
Stories
  Hazrat Bāyazīd Bistāmī proclaims, "I am God!" 7-10
  Insult proves the power of words, 23
  Lion thinks he's a donkey, 33-34
  Nasruddīn uses a flashlight to look for the sun, 15
  Seeker tries not to think of a monkey, 19-20
Suffering, 6
Sukhāsana (easy posture), 26
Sun, inner, 28
Sundardās, 16

Thoughts, 18, 19-22 32, 36, 37
Time, for meditation, 35
Transcendent state, 29
Transformation, 4
Truth, absolute, 13, 17, 23, 28
  search for, 2
Tukārām, 22
Turīya (transcendent state), 29

Understanding, 36
  of Consciousness, 32
  deepening of, 6
  mantra and, 24
  meditation and, 34, 37
  mind and, 22
  Self and, 7, 13, 15
  wrong, 2-3, 32, 34
Universe
  Blue Pearl and, 30
  Consciousness and, 11, 20-21, 32
  inner, 27-28
  mantra and, 24
  meditation and, 5
  Self and, 31, 34
  See also World
Upaniṣads, 1, 4
  on God, 13
  on meditation, 5
  on mind, 20
  on Self-realization, 12
  on Witness-consciousness, 17
Utpaladeva, 32

Vasiṣṭha, 13
Vedānta
  on false identification, 33-34
  on meditation, 28
  on pain and pleasure, 6
Vijñāna Bhairava, 13
Visions, in meditation, 37

Weariness, 2
Witness-consciousness, 7, 17, 21-22, 36
Words, 22-24
World, 11, 37
  See also Universe
Worldly life, 1-2, 4-5, 23
Worlds, inner, 6, 28
Worship, 27

Yoga-sūtra (Patañjali), 16, 25

Further Study

PUBLISHED BY THE SYDA FOUNDATION

Selected Books by Swami Muktānanda

BHAGAWAN NITYANANDA OF GANESHPURI

Swami Muktānanda's intimate account of the life and teachings of his Guru, Bhagavān Nityānanda, whose essential teaching is "The Heart is the hub of all sacred places. Go there and roam."

FROM THE FINITE TO THE INFINITE

As Swami Muktānanda traveled the world, seekers from many countries asked question after question about their spiritual practices. With profound insight and compassionate humor, Bābā answered them. This volume contains a wealth of those exchanges, offering readers the opportunity to recognize their own questions and to contemplate Bābā's responses.

I AM THAT
The Science of Haṁsa from the Vijñāna Bhairava

In this commentary on verse 24 of the *Vijñāna Bhairava,* a classic text of the nondual Shaivism of Kashmir, Swami Muktānanda teaches about the power of the *Haṁsa* mantra. Bābā reveals the mystical secrets of this form of mantra repetition and explains how, through dedicated practice, one can become established in the unwavering experience of inner divinity.

KUṆḌALINĪ
The Secret of Life

The awakening of Kuṇḍalinī, the latent spiritual energy within us, marks the beginning of the journey to perfection. What is the nature of this divine force? How is it awakened? And how can its progress be nurtured? Swami Muktānanda addresses these questions, giving both philosophical and practical guidance.

MUKTESHWARI

These autobiographical verses are among Swami Muktānanda's earliest writings. In studying them, the reader engages with the mystical and practical subtleties of Siddha Yoga *sādhanā*.

PLAY OF CONSCIOUSNESS
A Spiritual Autobiography

This unique spiritual autobiography describes Swami Muktānanda's own process of inner transformation under the guidance of his Guru, Bhagavān Nityānanda. A rare opportunity to study the first-hand account of a Siddha Master's journey to Self-realization.

Selected Books by Gurumayi Chidvilāsānanda

COURAGE AND CONTENTMENT

Opening with Gurumayi's Siddha Yoga Message talk for 1997, *Wake Up to Your Inner Courage and Become Steeped in Divine Contentment,* this volume includes eight talks in which Gurumayi unfolds the subtle connections between courage and contentment. To face life's challenges with courage and yet to feel content no matter what happens—this is the fruit of ongoing spiritual practice. It is a fruit, Gurumayi teaches, that ripens with intention, constancy, and patience.

ENTHUSIASM

This volume includes talks Gurumayi gave on the Siddha Yoga Message for 1996, *Be Filled with Enthusiasm and Sing God's Glory.* "Seize the opportunity to discover boundless enthusiasm," Gurumayi tells us. "Let the practices of yoga unfold miraculous experiences for you." Gurumayi explores virtues such as patience, forgiveness, gentleness, service, and gratitude—all of which enable us to cultivate our innate enthusiasm and ultimately to perceive God's glory everywhere in every moment of our lives.

MY LORD LOVES A PURE HEART
The Yoga of Divine Virtues

In a series of commentaries on chapter 16 of the *Bhagavad-gītā*, Gurumayi offers precise guidance on how to manifest the magnificent virtues of fearlessness, purity of being, steadfastness, freedom from anger, respect, compassion, humility, and selfless service.

SĀDHANĀ OF THE HEART
Siddha Yoga Messages for the Year

Each talk in this collection was originally presented to Siddha Yoga students as a message for the year, and each one endures as a focus of contemplation and a source of revelation. These talks, shining with Gurumayi's wisdom and practical guidance, support a seeker's effort on the journey to the experience of the supreme Heart.

THE YOGA OF DISCIPLINE

By contemplating the talks in this volume, the reader learns how to cultivate yogic discipline and how to apply it to everyday activities. Chapters include Gurumayi's discussions on how to bring yogic discipline to seeing, listening, eating, speaking, and thinking, so that we can "break through boundaries and reach the highest goal."

MEDITATION INSTRUCTIONS (recording)

In this audio recording Gurumayi gives meditation instructions that carry the listener naturally into meditation. In each of the meditation sessions on the recording, Gurumayi gives guidance on posture, breath, and mantra repetition for all levels of meditators. Gurumayi tells us, "Begin your meditation with absolute conviction. It is your right to perceive your own divine light within."

To learn more about
the Siddha Yoga teachings and practices,
visit the Siddha Yoga path website at:

www.siddhayoga.org

For further information about
SYDA Foundation books
and audio, video, and DVD recordings,
visit the Siddha Yoga Bookstore website at:

www.siddhayogabookstore.org

or call 845-434-2000, extension 1700.

From the United States and Canada,
call toll-free 888-422-3334.